How to Teach Your Kid Responsibility

Powerful Techniques for Getting Your Kid to Behave, Learn and Grow into A Self-Reliant Adult

By

Ann R. Sutton

Table of Contents

Introduction

For the fact that you are influencing a new experience to a new life, parenting could also be among the hardest jobs on earth. Nevertheless, it is almost very easy to achieve a specific goal concerning raising a kid once a specific goal is being set. It is very important to note that different form of effort is demanded to achieve a different goal, all depending on the age of the kid. You are responsible to making your kid ready for the outside world, the way they perceive it, how they react and the kind of respect they derive.

Responsibility is one of the most important qualities a person can adapt in the early stage of growth. It shapes the kid fast and exposes him to better opportunities. Your child will automatically become independent and you won't need to deal with common teenage problems, such as rebellion. This is all about raising a responsible kid.

Your parenting skills will never be the same after reading this book to the last page. You will learn the basic tips and tricks every parents supposed to apply in order to expand their kids understanding on the importance of practicing responsible behaviors. They will learn the essence of learning in correspondent to the growth they will experience even as they pursue education both at school, in the street, and within the confinement of your home.

Just the way a kid has to learn baseball, responsibility is adapted through learning and consistent practice. A kid has to be exposed to the literal learning of the importance and application of responsibility in order to be responsible. Also, responsibility is not limited to following instructions or attempting to do good. It is also knowing the reason to do the right things and finding motivations to do them without the supervision of an adult.

The Response

Presently, you don't have to change on your kid by assuming control all of a sudden. Regardless of their age or level of maturity, kids can rebel when they feel like they are being put under sudden control. In fact, control cultivates lies and deceptiveness in kids. If your kid behaves badly, go back to the book and provide the appropriate punishment in order to make them realize how bad they've been behaving.

Punishing them above the level of offence will not build a responsible kid. You have to be careful when it comes to creating consequences when kids misbehave. Sometimes it is best advised that you allow natural consequences to occur when kids refuse to follow your instructions.

For example, when your instruction is to simply help them to make adjustments so they will avoid something, allow them to experience the things you are protecting them from. You will by then notice the effect of willingness when it comes to following strict instructions and being creative about a work process.

Always use logical consequences in order to put your kids on the straight and narrow. You don't always have to use the same method of punishment either. The experienced parents have long ago adopted the deal method as a form of motivation to kids, to push them to finish chores or tasks. You may decide to not do what they want you to do until they prove to be good for a week or two. This will provide a thinking platform where

responsibility will come into play.

Be Patient and Allow Them to Respond

Some kids can be really slow in responding to instructions. You have to be patient enough to allow them to respond accordingly. Some will not follow through all the way, doing the things instructed, and you would need to correct them consistently. You have to be able to be patient enough to correct them several times.

Also, avoid repetition when it comes to giving instructions. One of the common mistakes most parents make is repeating a sentence up to 5 times hoping that the number of times repeated will provide an emphasis, making the kid to act fast or accordingly.

But according to an experiment, parents who say things once and clearly tend to achieve better score in raising a responsible kid than parents who repeat the same things over and over again. Inasmuch as your kid can hear and understand you clearly, state your request and be patient enough to allow them to respond.

So, it is of great advantage to give your kid an opportunity to feel the need for responsibility right within. By saying things only once, you are indirectly telling your kid that you believe they can be responsible and respond to a single instruction. If your kid doesn't respond you can allow the consequences to go on or you can inflict the required consequences. Next time, your kid will know that you mean what you mean

when you say things just once, and they

will follow through.

Ignore Them to Instill Sense

You don't have to be stiff or respond to every little irrational or inappropriate behavior. You have to be calm down and allow things to go naturally. Repeatedly, allowing natural consequences to befall them is one of the best ways you can allow your kid to learn and be responsible for their actions. It is very important to make them understand what happens when some things are not being done at all, done perfectly, or done at the required time.

Teaching responsibility to a kid could be difficult if they don't know the essence of making the right choices and executing correctly the required task. You will find out that most kids have some character traits that you may not be able to change. For example, most kids complain, easily forgetful, procrastinate and may whine when they feel stressed.

These are among the behaviors you can ignore especially when done casually and inconsistently. Do not give kids extra attention for this behaviors, because it will only encourage them to do their worse in exhibiting such characteristics.

Although most parents find it hard to ignore some of these behaviors, you have to be strong enough to observe the progress you are making to your emotions and to your parenting skills, and you will surely find reasons to ignore them even as you enjoy the new territory.

Also, you have to ignore a certain behavior now, make sure that you also ignore it later. You have to be consistent about it, and make sure your kids know your present stance when it comes to their behavior.

This way they would know that complaining and whining is not the best way to get your attention. Also in the cases of disputes, you have to allow kids to learn how to solve things within themselves. Being always at the aid will help your kids in learning how to deal with pressure, solving problems, and

even reconnecting within themselves.

Create an Alternation

Instead of punishing them for not behaving well, actually provide a suggestion for the things they should be doing instead of fighting or jumping all over the place. Sometimes kids just need a better option in order to be calm and start behaving.

There is no need to keep shouting on your kids when they are fighting, when you can just suggest a sweet game for them to automatically forget about the squabble. This has been among the most interesting experimented form of parenting that worked like magic.

According to the study, most parents may not feel the need to be nice, suggestive or even creative when kids are misbehaving, but those that are strong enough to suggest the better activity tend to end up happier, and the kids will improve faster.

The Behavior of the Responsible

There are certain ways responsible people act, respond and even execute actions or decisions. Do not hesitate to reinforce such behaviors and actions in your kids early in life.

This begins by paying attention to what your kids are doing. You have to actualize exactly the places your kids are strong, the places they tend to ignore, and the places they are totally weak.

You have to give more attention to the positive sides of their behaviors and less attention to the negative. It is very important that a kid notices that he can gain a better attention by doing the right thing instead of doing the wrong things.

Always take the time to praise your kids through words or physical awards. Make them feel special just for making an effort to do the simplest right things. Also, you could integrate this by totally ignoring your kid when they are misbehaving and by giving them immediate attention and praises on the next good things you will catch them doing.

Stepping out and Stepping in

Actually step back and allow your kids to do the best. You don't need to be on constant supervision of the things they do. Kids need to feel like you believe in them, the decisions they make and how capable they are in following simple instructions.

Once the importance of carrying out a task is made clear, parents are advised to leave the premises. Or to allow their kids to know that they are not being consistently supervised. You need to give them a breathing space to be creative about the whole work process.

On the other hand, when you feel ignored by your kid, you don't have to react immediately. Surprise them by stepping back and relaxing just like nothing has happened. Give them the chance to get on the way, or allow the natural consequence to take over.

The Rewards System Mistakes

Even though rewards are a great way to motivate your kid to do the right things, you have to use reward wisely in order to not spoil the kid instead of motivating him to do the right things. Some parents feel the need to give their kids something every time they finished a given task, and thus the kids feel the need to be given a reward every time they are asked to do something.

Rewards are only relevant when a kid reach a milestone; when a kid was able to finish a task faster or reached a level of accomplishment that has never been reached before.

You have to teach you kids the importance of doing stuff and not just the reward of doing stuff. There is a reason we clean the sink, there is a reason we take the garbage bag outside, there is a reason we do the laundry and if we don't do those things, there are consequences awaiting us.

Teach your kids responsibility from the angle of reasons, not from the angle of reward. They just need rewards from time to time motivation, to be shown that they are actually appreciated for doing it better than other kids. Also, let there be consistency on the specific work a kid is expected to perform.

Once it is understood that people don't get rewarded with gifts or money for the things they do around the house, your kid will not be expecting a reward every time he does something.

Also, find a way to differentiate the responsibilities they have to take for themselves and the responsibilities they take to help everyone. Starting from personal hygiene to taking a step towards improving their soccer skills, kids will learn the differences between taking responsibilities and doing the right things, and combining both to make life easier.

Known Responsibilities and Their Application

At different level of growth, your kid should know their responsibility and the responsibilities of others. Being responsible is not just about doing stuff, it is also about knowing what the other person supposed to do and why they should do them.

On the reasons they have to take responsibilities, kids supposed to derive motivation from the other members of the family. So it is very important to lay down or delegate for each member of the family the things they supposed to do and let that be known by the kids. You can discuss this on the dinner table.

This will provide the sense of teamwork, and your kids will be even glad to take their own responsibility as a challenge to be as good as you are or the other person seating around the table. Regardless how small and simple, laying out responsibilities is important in creating a healthy sense of self especially in kids.

Age appropriate

According to the study, one of the most important parenting skills for a parent to recognize and assign "age appropriate" tasks to kids. You have to know when your kid is too old for some tasks, and promote them to tougher and more challenging tasks. Also, you have to know when your kid is too young to do some stuff, so you won't expose them to danger.

Do not allow toddlers to handle things that may cause harm. Do not let them near the kitchen inasmuch as there are knives, the gas and everything. Allow them to dust stuff, and/or even wash their hands. When they become older they might begin setting the dinner table, emptying the vacuum, dishwasher etc.

Allow them to be different

Kids tend to be creative at their early stage of life. Encourage their creativity. That is the only way they will differentiate between the essence of responsibility and the obligation behind it. They will find a territory of their own where they will stand out and actually raise above all odds of childishness.

Thus they would become young adults earlier. Kids that cannot stand out find it hard to create balance between the feeling of obligation and actually taking known responsibilities.

Do not blame

Let the atmosphere of your home be about harmony and finishing things. Do not resort to blame when things are not going well. Always focus on fixing problems and let the kids learn these characteristics from you. Pushing blames around is a kind of escape from responsibility that even adults practice.

Make sure that you don't teach your kids how to escape from responsibility in an attempt to make yourself look superior. Always fix things, even though you know who is at a fault. Only correct when you can, and move on from there.

Expose them to payment

At a certain stage of life, basically early teen, kids could be exposed to tasks that might earn them direct money. You can volunteer for a day or two to take them to your workplace or to some manual business where your kids will know exactly the amount of effort needed in order to make money.

This would absolutely hone their money responsibility. They will begin to think about money differently, and they will ultimately learn to be creative in order to earn instead of continuously asking for money.

One of the best form of responsibility in the world is money responsibility. You will be glad when your kid learns this early in life.

Go Positive

It is very important to make sure your kid is responsible, but do not call them irresponsible anytime they fail. Make sure you allow them to know their mistakes, and support them even as they begin to correct things. Do not underestimate the power of autosuggestion.

Negativity can be transmuted and your kid might actually respond in accordance to your labelling. So, never ever call your kid names that depicts the opposite of what you would desire. Teach them how to be better. This is the main reason why it is called parenting—teaching, guiding, correcting, encouraging, instructing, and loving.